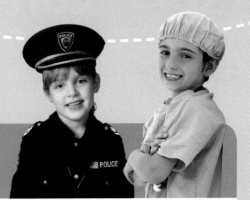

What's in this book

This book belongs to

_____

职业日 Career Day

学习内容 Contents

沟通 Communication

谈一谈职业
Talk about jobs

生词 New words

★	老师	teacher
★	工作	job, work
★	警察	police officer
★	服务员	waiter, waitress
★	律师	lawyer
★	办公室	office
★	司机	driver
★	能	to be able to
	上班	to go to work
	下班	to get off work
	先生	sir, Mr
	小姐	Miss

他的爸爸是司机，能天天开车去不同的地方。

His father is a driver. He can drive to different places every day.

万世师表——孔子

The teacher for all ages—Confucius

使用思维导图组织信息，并发表演讲

Use a mind map to organize ideas and make a speech

Get ready

1 Can you name any jobs that are related to our everyday lives?

2 What do you think is the most interesting job?

3 What does Hao Hao's father do?

gōng zuò
工作

lǎo shī
老师

今天是学校的职业日，老师请了很多家长来介绍他们的工作。

上班 shàng bān

下班 xià bān

警察 jǐng chá

她的爸爸是警察。他很早上班，很晚下班。

他的妈妈是服务员。她很喜欢笑，常常说："先生，您好！小姐，您好！"

律师 lǜ shī

办公室 bàn gōng shì

她的妈妈是律师。她在办公室上班，工作很多、很忙。

他的爸爸是司机，能天天开车去
不同的地方。

工作真有趣！我长大了想像爸爸
一样，做一名老师，传授知识。

Let's think

1 Recall the story. Match the parents to their workplaces.

2 Sometimes your small acts could make a big difference to other people's work. Discuss with your friend what you should do in the following situations.

New words

1 Learn the new words.

服务员

先生

警察

律师

司机

小姐

能
be able to

老师

办公室

工作

上班

下班

2 Listen to your friend and point to the correct words above.

1 Listen and circle the correct letters.

1 他的妈妈的工作是什么？

a 司机

b 律师

c 服务员

2 她的奶奶能做什么？

a 踢足球

b 说汉语

c 上网

3 中文老师每天几点休息？

a 三点半

b 七点

c 十点

2 Look at the pictures. Listen to the story

① 爸爸，您下班了！

爸爸，您看，布朗尼是个小"司机"。

③ 小姐、先生们，喝点果汁吧，休息休息。

谢谢玲玲，你是最好的"服务员"。

它能开车了，你们应该很高兴。

是啊，我们是它的老师。

我去做饭了。

妈妈的工作真多，我们一起帮助您，好吗？

Talk about the pictures with your friend.

1

她是医生，她能做什么？

她能……

2

他是……
你想做……吗？

我……

3

你知道老师几点上班、几点下班吗？

……

Task

What are your family members' jobs and what do you want to do when you grow up? Draw hints in the family tree. Work with your friend to ask and answer questions about the jobs.

Game

Act out the jobs and ask your friend to guess them in Chinese.

Chant

 Listen and say.

当我们长大了，要工作，要工作。
我想成为老师，天天在学校。
我也想成为司机，天天开车。

当我们长大了，要工作，要工作。
我想成为律师，律师能帮助人。
我想成为警察，警察也能帮助人。

当我们长大了，要工作，要工作。
我想成为医生，或者护士，
或者服务员。

生活用语 Daily expressions

对不起!
Sorry!

没关系。
It's OK.

写一写 Write

1 Trace and write the characters.

一 十 土 耂 耂 老
丿 刂 阝 阝 师 师

老 师 | 老 师

老 师

一 丁 工
丿 亻 亻 仁 仁 作 作

工 作 | 工 作

工 作

2 Write and say.

数学 ＿＿＿＿
在上课。

爸爸很喜欢他
的新 ＿＿＿＿＿。

3 Read and circle the correct words.

妹妹的数学（很好/不好），她长大了想做个数学（老师/律师）。（放学/下班）了，她喜欢在花园里给小狗上数学课。妹妹真（可爱/生气）！我觉得她能做一个好（老师/律师）。

拼音输入法 Pinyin input

Complete the passage and write the letters. Then work with your friend and type the whole passage.

a 妈妈很忙。　　b 星期日，妈妈不上班。　　c 妈妈很好看。

这是我的妈妈。

___她个子不高，脸圆圆的，很爱笑。大家都很喜欢她。

___她是个护士，在医院上班。她早上六点半起床，晚上十二点休息。

___我们一起运动、看书和做蛋糕，真快乐！

我爱妈妈！

多元学习 Connections

Cultures

1 Confucius is regarded as 'the teacher for all ages' in China. Learn about him.

孔子（kǒng zǐ）是我们的老师。

Confucius (551–479 BC) was a famous Chinese teacher and philosopher.

He promoted the ideas of *ren*, *yi* and *li*.

rén 仁 *Ren*, benevolence. One should be kind and love others.

yì 义 *Yi*, righteousness. One should have more principles and do good things.

lǐ 礼 *Li*, propriety. One should have good manners and follow the rules.

Many of Confucius' philosophy and ideas on education were recorded as conversations between him and his students in *The Analects*.

2 Read the sayings about learning from *The Analects*. Discuss with your friend what they mean.

三个人一起走，里面有我的老师。

The Master said, 'When I walk along with two others, they may serve me as my teachers.'

The Master said, 'If a man keeps cherishing his old knowledge, so as continually to be acquiring new, he may be a teacher of others.'

为什么？

1. Imagine that you are 28 years old and you are going to make a speech about your job. Look at the mind map and draw your own one to include the points that you want to talk about in your speech.

我是……

我在……

我能……

我……上班，
……下班。

下班了，
我……

2. Now make a speech. Use the information in your mind map.

温习 Checkpoint

1 What does each person in this building do? Read aloud what they say and solve their riddles. Help the woman find her friend.

我是律师，天天都很晚下班。

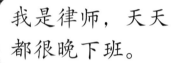

我是护士。

我的 ☐☐ 是帮助生病的人。

我也能帮助生病的人。我是……

我能天天开车，去不同的地方。我是……

我天天说："您想吃什么？"我是……

我的工作是帮助这个城市的人。我是……

我在学校上课。

我是 ☐☐。

我的朋友是医生，住在第＿＿层的（左边/中间/右边）。

我在家上班。我的卧室也是我的办公室。

左边　　　　　中间　　　　　右边

2 Work with your friend. Colour the stars and the chillies.

Words	说	读	写
老师	☆	☆	☆
工作	☆	☆	☆
警察	☆	☆	🌶
服务员	☆	☆	🌶
律师	☆	☆	🌶
办公室	☆	☆	🌶
司机	☆	☆	🌶
能	☆	☆	🌶

Words and sentences	说	读	写
上班	☆	🌶	🌶
下班	☆	🌶	🌶
先生	☆	🌶	🌶
小姐	☆	🌶	🌶
他的爸爸是司机，能天天开车去不同的地方。	☆	🌶	🌶

Talk about jobs	☆

3 What does your teacher say?

My teacher says ...

分享 Sharing

Words I remember

老师	lǎo shī	teacher
工作	gōng zuò	job, work
警察	jǐng chá	police officer
服务员	fú wù yuán	waiter, waitress
律师	lǜ shī	lawyer
办公室	bàn gōng shì	officer
司机	sī jī	driver
能	néng	to be able to
上班	shàng bān	to go to work
下班	xià bān	to get off work
先生	xiān sheng	sir, Mr
小姐	xiǎo jiě	Miss

Other words

职业日	zhí yè rì	career day
请	qǐng	to invite
家长	jiā zhǎng	parents
早	zǎo	early
晚	wǎn	late
常常	cháng cháng	often
有时	yǒu shí	sometimes
天天	tiān tiān	every day
开车	kāi chē	to drive
有趣	yǒu qù	interesting
长大	zhǎng dà	to grow up
名	míng	(measure word)
传授	chuán shòu	to pass on
知识	zhī shi	knowledge

OXFORD
UNIVERSITY PRESS

Oxford University Press is a department of the University of Oxford.
It furthers the University's objective of excellence in research, scholarship,
and education by publishing worldwide. Oxford is a registered trade mark of
Oxford University Press in the UK and in certain other countries

Published in Hong Kong by
Oxford University Press (China) Limited
39th Floor, One Kowloon, 1 Wang Yuen Street, Kowloon Bay,
Hong Kong

Illustrated by Ah Lun, Anne Lee, Emily Chan, KY Chan and Wildman

Photographs for reproduction permitted by Dreamstime.com

China National Publications Import & Export (Group) Corporation is an authorized distributor of
Oxford Elementary Chinese.

Please contact content@cnpiec.com.cn or 86-10-65856782

ISBN: 978-0-19-082310-8

10 9 8 7 6 5 4 3 2